T0395085

Slithering Snakes

DIAMONDBACK RATTLESNAKE

NORTH AMERICAN HUNTER

BY NATALIE HUMPHREY

Enslow
PUBLISHING

DISCOVER!

Please visit our website, www.enslow.com. For a free color catalog of all our high-quality books, call toll free 1-800-398-2504 or fax 1-877-980-4454.

Cataloging-in-Publication Data

Names: Humphrey, Natalie.
Title: Diamondback rattlesnake: North American hunter / Natalie Humphrey.
Description: New York : Enslow Publishing, 2021. | Series: Slithering snakes | Includes glossary and index.
Identifiers: ISBN 9781978517752 (pbk.) | ISBN 9781978517776 (library bound) | ISBN 9781978517769 (6 pack)
Subjects: LCSH: Eastern diamondback rattlesnake—Juvenile literature. | Western diamondback rattlesnake—Juvenile literature.
Classification: LCC QL666.O69 H85 2021 | DDC 597.96'38—dc23

Published in 2021 by
Enslow Publishing
101 West 23rd Street, Suite #240
New York, NY 10011

Designer: Sarah Liddell
Editor: Natalie Humphrey

Photo credits: Cover, p. 1 (diamondback rattlesnake) Matt Jeppson/Shutterstock.com; background pattern used throughout Ksusha Dusmikeeva/Shutterstock.com; background texture used throughout Lukasz Szwaj/Shutterstock.com; p. 5 R. Andrew Odum/Photodisc/Getty Images; p. 7 David Bose/500Px Plus/Getty Images; p. 9 Bob Jensen/500Px Plus/Getty Images; p. 11 Danita Delimont/Gallo Images/Getty Images Plus/Getty Images; p. 13 Brian Magnier/iStock/Getty Images Plus/Getty Images; p. 15 Mark Kostich/Shutterstock.com; p. 17 Pat Gaines/Moment/Getty Images; p. 19 kristianbell/RooM/Getty Images; p. 21 boreala/Shutterstock.com.

Portions of this work were originally authored by Autumn Leigh and published as *Diamondback Rattlesnake*. All new material this edition authored by Natalie Humphrey.

Printed in the United States of America

Some of the images in this book illustrate individuals who are models. The depictions do not imply actual situations or events.

CPSIA compliance information: Batch #BS20ENS: For further information contact Enslow Publishing, New York, New York, at 1-800-398-2504.

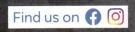

CONTENTS

Deadly Diamondbacks 4

East and West 6

Shades and Shapes 10

Baby Diamondbacks 12

A Snake That Rattles 14

Diamondback Attack! 16

Diamondbacks and People . . 20

Words to Know 22

For More Information 23

Index 24

Boldface words appear in Words to Know.

DEADLY DIAMONDBACKS

Known for their trademark rattle and the diamond pattern on their back, diamondback rattlesnakes are dangerous **predators**! Often just called diamondbacks, they live in warm places across southern North America. During the winter, diamondbacks hide in their **dens** and **hibernate** until it's warm again!

DIAMONDBACK
RATTLESNAKE

5

EAST AND WEST

There are two types of diamondbacks. Eastern diamondbacks are found in the Southeast, from Louisiana all the way up to North Carolina. Western diamondbacks are found in the Southwest and range from Texas to central Mexico. Both types have a rattle on their tail and sharp **fangs**.

DIAMONDBACKS CAN LIVE IN THE WILD FOR 15 TO 20 YEARS!

7

Diamondbacks are big rattlesnakes. Adult diamondbacks are around 5 feet (1.5 m) long and weigh around 10 pounds (4.5 kg). The eastern diamondback can grow much larger than the western. Some eastern diamondbacks have grown up to 8 feet (2.4 m) long and weighed 15 pounds (7 kg)!

DIAMONDBACKS ARE THE LARGEST VENOMOUS SNAKES IN THE UNITED STATES.

SHADES AND SHAPES

Diamondbacks come in many different colors. They all have diamond-shaped **patterns** along their back. They can be black, gray, brown, red, yellow, or green. A diamondback's colors help it blend into its home. Western diamondbacks have black and white stripes just above their rattle.

DIAMONDBACKS ALSO HAVE DIAMOND-SHAPED HEADS.

BABY DIAMONDBACKS

During the summer, female diamondbacks give birth to between 4 and 32 babies. Baby diamondbacks are born with venom, and their bite is just as dangerous as that of a full-grown rattlesnake! They use their venom to stay safe and hunt small prey.

DIAMONDBACK MOTHERS LEAVE SOON AFTER THEIR BABIES ARE BORN.

13

A SNAKE THAT RATTLES

All snakes shed their skin as they grow, but rattlesnakes have one extra step! When a rattlesnake sheds, a tiny piece of skin remains on the tip of its tail. Each time it sheds, more pieces build up until the rattle is made!

THE FIRST PIECE OF A DIAMONDBACK'S RATTLE IS CALLED A BUTTON.

DIAMONDBACK ATTACK!

Diamondbacks are pit vipers. Pit vipers have extra holes, called pits, behind their noses. When a diamondback is hunting, its colors and markings help it hide. Using its pits, the snake senses the heat of passing animals. When its prey gets too close, the diamondback **attacks**!

PIT

When a diamondback is ready to attack, it goes into a special pose. It lifts the front of its body off the ground and makes an S shape. The diamondback bites its prey and shoots venom into the animal's body. Once the animal is dead, the rattlesnake swallows it whole!

DIAMONDBACKS EAT SMALL RODENTS AND BIRDS.

DIAMONDBACKS AND PEOPLE

Diamondbacks are shy snakes and don't really want to be around people. If they see a person nearby, they'll shake their rattle as a warning. Diamondbacks bite only if they're surprised or nervous. If you hear a diamondback's rattle, stay as far away as you can!

WHERE DO DIAMONDBACK RATTLESNAKES LIVE?

NORTH AMERICA

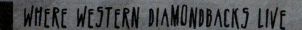 WHERE WESTERN DIAMONDBACKS LIVE

 WHERE EASTERN DIAMONDBACKS LIVE

21

WORDS TO KNOW

attack To try to harm someone or something.

den A wild animal's hidden home.

fang A long, sharp tooth.

hibernate To spend the winter sleeping or resting.

pattern A repeated form or design.

predator An animal that lives by killing and eating other animals.

rodent A small animal, such as a mouse, rat, or squirrel, that has sharp front teeth.

venomous Able to make a liquid called venom that is harmful to other animals.

FOR MORE INFORMATION

BOOKS

Rathburn, Betsy. *Diamondback Rattlesnakes*. Minnetonka, MN: Blastoff! Readers, 2018.

Sprott, Gary. *Western Diamondback Rattlesnake*. Vero Beach, FL: Rourke Educational Media, 2018.

WEBSITES

National Geographic
www.nationalgeographic.com/animals/reptiles/e/eastern-diamondback-rattlesnake/
Check out more photographs of diamondback rattlesnakes!

Smithsonian's National Zoo & Conservation Biology Institute
nationalzoo.si.edu/animals/eastern-diamondback-rattlesnake
Discover more fun facts about eastern diamondbacks!

Publisher's note to educators and parents: Our editors have carefully reviewed these websites to ensure that they are suitable for students. Many websites change frequently, however, and we cannot guarantee that a site's future contents will continue to meet our high standards of quality and educational value. Be advised that students should be closely supervised whenever they access the internet.

INDEX

baby diamondbacks, 12

colors, 10, 16

dens, 4

eastern diamondbacks, 6, 8

fangs, 6

hibernate, 4

hiding, 4, 16

hunting, 12, 16, 18

patterns/markings, 4, 10, 16

pits, 16

pit vipers, 16

prey, 12, 16, 18

rattle, 4, 6, 10, 14, 20

shedding skin, 14

size, 8

venom, 12, 18

weight, 8

western diamondbacks, 6, 8, 10

where they are found, 4, 6